A Lamb
is Born

Looking out,
I saw a man approaching our abode,
Walking with his little beast,
on which a woman rode

To Brenda
Blessings
Stanley Annett

A Lamb Is Born and Other Poems © Shirley Amendt
Story Poems from the Life of Christ, from the Manger to the Cross,
Pentecost, and Paul

ISBN: 978-0-578-11322-7

Cover art by Stewart Sherwood; cover design by Dugan Design.

Published through BelieversPress.
Printed in USA by Bethany Press International.

A Lamb
is Born

AND OTHER POEMS

Story Poems from the Life of Christ
From the Manger to the Cross,
Pentecost, and Paul

By
Shirley Amendt

DEDICATION

I dedicate these poems to my Lord and Savior, Jesus Christ.

I wish to thank my husband for listening to every poem many times over and still encouraging me to write more. I also want to thank my son for his computer expertise, without which this manuscript would not exist, and my daughter for her overwhelming enthusiasm for my work. Also, I thank the many friends who listened and encouraged me unfailingly.

TABLE OF CONTENTS

"They knelt beside that manger and whispered their great joy!
Our Savior's born, and this is He, this little baby boy!"

*And they came with haste, and found Mary, and Joseph, and the babe
lying in a manger.*

Luke 2:16 KJV

A LAMB IS BORN

It happened while Augustus reigned, a decree came down from Rome.
All men must be registered in their ancestral home.

Boaz was of David's house; we lived in Bethlehem,
No journey for us was needed, to serve those mighty men.

We knew that weary travelers soon would flood our town;
We worked until we knew our inn was as good as could be found.

They crowded into Bethlehem all that whole long day;
Pushing, searching everywhere, to find a place to stay.

Boaz did his morning work; went out in the afternoon,
I finished up my wifely chores and rented every room.

When he came home, he smiled and said, 'he'd sold our temple lambs'.
We raised them just for sacrifice, and there was now a great demand.

He gave some travelers our own bed, and I wondered where we'd sleep.
He said that we should trust our God, and he sat down with them to eat.

Boaz dozed by the kitchen fire, untroubled by his cares.
I thought I'd check the gates and locks before I joined him there.

Looking out, I saw a man approaching our abode,
Walking with his little beast, on which a woman rode.

A LAMB IS BORN

It was late, and now quite dark when I unlocked the door.
Our inn was closed, the beds were full, with children on the floor.

"There's no room here." I said to them. "Try further down the street."
"We've tried them all and you're the last." Her pleading voice was sweet.

"Please," he said. "My wife is tired. She needs a place to rest.
She's near her time and must lie down; we'll take whatever's left."

She glanced down at the telling bulge beneath her cloak and gown.
This girl had need of a private place somewhere in this town.

I looked close, and saw the pain, etched across her face--
She quickly smiled, and then I said, "I think I know a place."

"It may be nothing you would want, but I'll show you a place to go--"
Their eyes lit up and they followed me, though her steps were very slow.

"It's just a stable in a cave--a birthing place for sheep.
There's bedding hay that's fresh and dry so she can get some sleep."

"It's quiet here, out of the wind, the sheep will keep you warm.
Many a night I've spent in here to help a lamb get born."

"It's good" he said, "You have our thanks. Now Mary can lie down.
There really was no other place left in this whole town!"

I held the lamp as he piled hay to make a soft sweet bed.
He pulled a blanket over her, his cloak beneath her head.

I brought them food, an evening meal, but only Joseph ate.
She slowly drank some water, but her pains did not abate.

It seemed that she might need some help, and I feared to leave her there.
I'd never even leave a sheep to birth without my care.

She seemed so young, with so much pain, my duty seemed quite clear.
"I'll stay and help you birth this lamb. I will be right here."

A LAMB IS BORN

I stayed close by, to wait with them through the chilly night.
We watched a star light up the cave with a softly glowing light!

He stroked her hair, he talked and prayed, to help her bear the pain.
She squeezed his hands and bit her lips so she could stand the strain.

With a gasping sob and a mighty push she at last brought forth her son!
She then lay back exhausted, pleased her work was done.

Joseph kissed her forehead and he gently squeezed her hand,
"The babe is here," he whispered. "Just as God has planned."

She watched us caring for her child, she loved him with her eyes.
Joseph held him in his arms and soothed his baby cries.

We rubbed him dry and swaddled him in linen soft and warm.
He laid the baby next to her in the cradle of her arms.

The child soon stopped his crying in her close embrace.
Joseph watched the baby nursing with wonder on his face.

I helped him care for Mary, made her bed more soft and deep.
We tucked the blanket close around and she drifted off to sleep.

Joseph filled the manger that was close by Mary's head.
He stuffed it full of grasses, and he made a little bed.

He lined the nest with strips of cloth, from a tunic soft and old,
And he laid the baby in it, sheltered from the cold.

Boaz came to the stable, and he brought a warming drink.
His wife was gone so long he said, he wondered what to think.

He looked down at the sleeping babe, and tears were on his face,
To think a new life had begun, here in this humble place.

He stayed with me while Joseph slept, lest the child should wake and cry,
Then shepherds came and told a tale, of angels in the sky!

An angel told them where to go, and what was waiting there--
A baby in a manger, wrapped up with loving care!

Joseph smiled and listened, his eyes were shining bright,
"There is a baby here!" he said. "Born this very night!"

They knelt beside that manger and whispered their great joy!
Our Savior's born, and this is He, this little baby boy!

They gazed at Him, and so did I, and then they went away,
Singing, yes, and praising God, for the miracle of this day!

A miracle--this newborn babe? We looked up at the sky!
And there were angels everywhere singing from on high!

"Glory, glory, glory to God, and peace to men on earth!"
Music come down from heaven to proclaim His holy birth.

We knelt down on that hard stone floor to worship God above,
And to thank Him that our stable was the cradle for His love.

In my heart I understood, what I hadn't known before,
This night, this child, had been a gift, from God to men, forevermore.

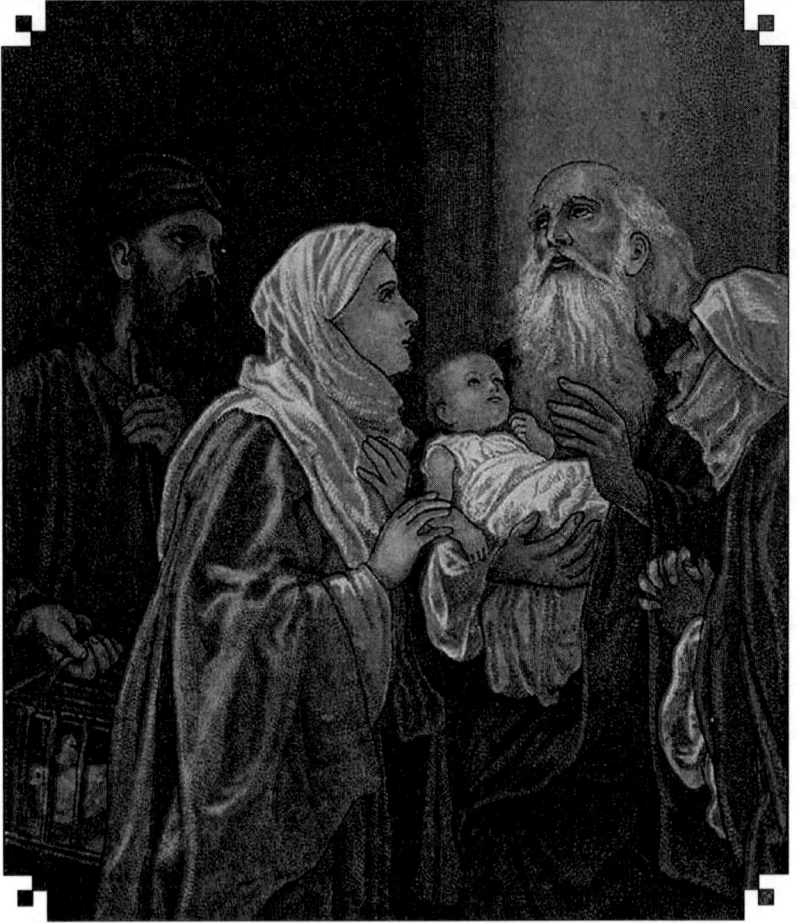

"Simeon, my friend for years, was standing with the three.
I knew that he heard angel songs; it wasn't only me!"

And she coming in that instant gave thanks likewise unto the Lord, and spake of him to all them that looked for redemption in Jerusalem.

Luke 2:38 KJV

ANNA
THE PROPHETESS

Somehow I've gotten very old; I've ceased to count my years.
I look back and see a life that was blessed with joy-- and tears.

I was given into marriage when I was seventeen.
He was a man my father knew, that I had never seen.

I grew to love him quickly, he was very good and kind,
I would have picked no other if the choosing had been mine.

We prayed that we'd have children, whatever God might give.
The first I lost at seven months, he was too small to live.

Still, I was young, and I let time heal my broken heart,
But in two years, I lost another; a failing on my part!

Isaiah was a patient man, he said that we'd have more.
He said it didn't matter, we would take it to the Lord.

We prayed and waited and prepared, for our child to come.
Every month I mourned anew, when again there wasn't one.

Six years had passed since Isaiah, took me for his wife,
And finally, I knew with joy, that in me there was life.

I felt so very sure this time, that all was going well.
Isaiah was a happy man, anyone could tell.

My husband brought me many gifts, clothing and perfume,
And together we arranged to have, a baby in our room.

In just one month we'd have a child, that we could touch and hold,
An active healthy boy or girl, that would bring us joy untold.

My husband left the house one day, he said he'd be back soon.
I went about my daily tasks, but he wasn't back by noon.

Then my father came to find me, and he said "Isaiah's dead".
Going down the temple steps, he fell and struck his head.

.

I couldn't make myself believe this thing that I'd been told,
Until they brought him back to me, lying still and cold.

And yet there was the baby, I'd bring forth in good time.
Very soon he would come and carry on Isaiah's line.

I held on tightly to this thought through the awful days ahead.
My mother came and stayed with me till I was brought to bed.

The baby came too early, but it was near the proper time.
I longed to hold my baby boy, Isaiah's child and mine.

Labor lasted many hours, it was a painful birth.
I didn't care how much I hurt, I knew my baby's worth.

God gave to me a little boy, the answer to our prayers.
When I held him close to me, it blotted out my cares.

And yet he was so tiny, and so weak he couldn't cry,
Deep down I knew the awful truth, but I told myself a lie.

My baby lived for just three days, before his life was taken.
I wanted so much to go with him, my very soul was shaken.

I left the house, no longer mine, and made the trip back home.
Mother was glad to have me there, but I needed time alone.

ANNA THE PROPHETESS

Father took me to the temple, though it was hard to pray.
Still it passed the dragging hours, so I went there every day.

I saw parents bringing baby sons, at the appointed time.
If things had just been different, I'd be bringing mine.

I loved to see those babies, but it made me weep inside.
I smiled and asked if I could help, and brushed my tears aside.

Sometimes a thought about the child, would come into my head,
And though I tried to hold it back, it seemed it must be said.

Helping in the temple, was the best part of my day,
Sometimes I minded children while their parents went to pray.

In a while, my father said, 'I should marry someone new'.
He brought some men to meet me, but none of them would do.

The men who came would notice that no children were around.
In seven years I'd not brought forth, a baby whole and sound.

I still loved Isaiah; I'd love him all my life.
I still loved our babies; I felt I was his wife.

I prayed at temple every day in the women's court;
I got to know the faithful, and I got to know the Lord.

I thought the Lord was telling me that I could serve him there;
And so I helped out where I could, and loved my time in prayer.

The Lord began to talk to me, and I got to know His voice.
When He told me what to say, I simply had no choice.

I spoke at first to women, to give comfort to their hearts.
I told them they could trust the Lord, to always do His part.

Then He bade me "speak" to men, though they must first ask me.
They wanted to know the Lord's will, whatever I could see.

A LAMB IS BORN

I told them what the Lord, had put into my mind.
I told them I knew nothing, that I was speaking blind.

It seemed my words were true enough; many sought me out.
Sometimes they called me "prophet" but I surely had my doubts.

This way of life continued, my day seemed carved in stone,
Till my mother and my father died, and left me quite alone.

My brother offered me a place, to come and live for life.
I tried it for a year or so, but it somehow wasn't right.

I seemed wedded to the temple, to fasting and to prayer.
If I left the temple ground, I wished I were still there.

The priests had come to be my friends, they all knew my name.
They felt the Lord was using me, and I felt much the same.

I lived there in the temple, to be nearer to my Lord,
And serve Him when He needed me, to speak His holy word.

The days passed by quickly, months and then the years.
My days were mostly happy, I was through with tears.

One winter morning I woke up, and knew that I'd grown old.
My thin and shaking body was shivering in the cold.

Yet now I felt a stirring, an excitement in my soul.
I felt that I was waiting for the Lord to make me whole.

I went to watch the parents as they brought their little boys.
I was glad to smile with them, and I loved to share their joys.

One young woman with her child, seemed to catch my eye.
She had a loving husband, who stayed close by her side.

He was gazing at the baby, then his eyes adored his wife.
There must be something wonderful, about His little life.

ANNA THE PROPHETESS

When I came and stood by them, they let me see His face.
Angel voices in my ears began singing songs of praise.

I opened up my mouth to speak, but not a word came out.
The angels joyful singing would have drowned out any shout.

Simeon, my friend for years, was standing with the three.
I knew that he heard angel songs; it wasn't only me!

Simeon had been waiting, so long to hold this child!
I listened to his solemn words, I heard and yet I smiled.

Simeon stood there with the baby, snuggled close and warm.
Tiny fingers' touched his face, while the child was in his arms.

His mother turned to look at me, with understanding eyes,
"Would you like to hold the babe?", she asked to my surprise.

I wrapped my arms around her, she welcomed my embrace.
I loved this girl, I loved this child, and I loved this time and place.

She put the baby in my arms, while those angels sang with joy.
For my whole long life I'd been waiting to hold this little boy.

Love and peace came over me, when I looked into His eyes.
I couldn't look away from Him, I had no desire to try.

When they left the temple, that early winter morn,
I knew I had to tell the news, a Savior has been born!

People come and people go, I tell them all the same,
The Messiah's born, He is on earth, and Jesus is His name!

As long as God will let me live, and I still have a voice,
I will proclaim the Christ child's birth, so we can all rejoice!

"The three men knelt there on the floor, looking closely at the Child. He opened wide His baby eyes, and they stared at Him, beguiled."

And when they were come into the house, they saw the young child with Mary his mother, and fell down, and worshipped him: and when they had opened their treasures, they presented unto him gifts; gold, and frankincense and myrrh.

Matthew 2:11 KJV

THE MAGI'S VISIT

Bethlehem grew quiet as the many travelers left.
Now our inn had empty rooms, but we were not bereft.

The couple in the stable had been struggling with the cold.
So they moved into the house, with a Baby we could hold.

Joseph planned to go back home, but he agreed with Mary.
The baby was so young, she said, it was better that they tarry.

Joseph was a carpenter, work came quickly to his hand.
A carpenter can work at home, or in any foreign land.

I hoped that they would stay and live with us in Bethlehem.
I dreamed that we could watch the Babe, till He grew into a man.

The winter days passed quickly, and we watched the Baby grow.
They would soon return to Nazareth, and they gently let us know.

Their families were living there, and we really understood,
To be living near your family, was something very good.

The building jobs that Joseph took, all were now complete.
Mary talked of Nazareth, and her dreams of home were sweet.

And still the star stayed in the sky, lighting up the night!
We had never seen a distant star, so glowing and so bright!

That evening, when the meal was done and the Babe lay fast asleep,
There were noises in the courtyard, and the bleating of the sheep.

Boaz hurried to the door, and out into the night.
I quickly followed after him, into that star's bright light.

Coming toward our dwelling were three men finely dressed.
They must be needing shelter, and I thought they would be guests.

Boaz went to speak with them, to invite them to come in.
We had water for their camels, food and lodging for the men.

One of them began to speak, and he pointed at the star.
"We have followed that!" he said. "And we have traveled far."

"A king's been born in Bethlehem, and the star has led us here.
We have come to see this Child. We are sure that He is near."

"I'll fetch the water," Boaz said, "and let your camels drink."
I knew that he just gave himself, a little time to think.

"My wife will take you in the house, where you can sit and rest.
My wife's spiced wine and barley cakes, are the city's best."

They smiled at that and followed me, as I led them to the inn.
I noticed the fine embroidered silk, in the clothing of these men.

Joseph waited by the fire, and the three men joined him there.
I warmed the wine and little cakes, and took the greatest care.

They began to speak to Joseph, and I heard their tale unfold;
"We have traveled many miles through summer heat and cold."

"The stars told us a king was born to rule this Jewish land.
He will be a mighty king with great power in his hand.

"We felt that God was leading us, to come and find Him here.
We have brought our finest gifts, the things that men hold dear."

Joseph seemed to hesitate, not knowing what to say.
He looked closely at the men, and then he looked away.

"God led you here?" he finally asked, with wonder in his voice.
"Yes," the tallest one replied. "We believe this is God's choice."

Joseph still was silent, doubt was written on his face,
Till Mary came into the room with sweet and silent grace.

"The babe is here," she softly said. "The one you've come to see.
When He was born the angels sang. God gave this Child to me."

She sat down beside the fire, the babe lay in her arms.
"I trust that having seen my Son, you will not bring Him harm."

The three men knelt there on the floor, looking closely at the Child.
He opened wide His baby eyes, and they stared at Him, beguiled.

"We would never harm this Babe; we are honest seeking men.
We've traveled many weary miles to come to Bethlehem."

One of the men reached in his gown, and drew out a leather bag.
"It's gold," he told her simply, as he laid it in her lap.

One handed Joseph frankincense, and the other one had myrrh.
"We have come to serve this King," one man said to her."

"God has brought you here," she said. "And now I must know why."
"What is the reason you were led by this star still in the sky?"

The three men looked at one another as though they would say more.
Then Boaz, finished with the camels, entered through the door.

"Tell them where you've been today, and who you talked to first."
Boaz looked them in the eye. "Just let them know the worst."

"I was speaking with your servant, as we gave your camels drink.
He said a lot of wondrous things, now I don't know what to think."

The tallest of the three of them, got slowly to his feet.
He looked around at all of us, and then began to speak.

"We went first to Herod's court, to find a newborn king.
We listened and we realized, they didn't know a thing.

We were told to find this Child, and come back to Herod's court.
If a king is born in Bethlehem, he must have a full report.

Herod told us his desire is to worship and to serve,
As any king of David's house, truly would deserve.

We left the court and Herod, and continued with the star,
Until it stopped and stayed here, exactly where we are."

I saw Mary was amazed, and Joseph struck with awe.
They stared at these fine strangers, unsure of what they saw!

"We still don't know," said Joseph "why you traveled here?
What is it that you plan to do? And what have we to fear?"

"We are men of learning, and we come from Eastern lands.
We seek to learn and follow God, and the working of His hands."

"We saw the star foretelling, a new King's coming birth.
We knew this King would rule someday, over all the earth."

"We've traveled here to find Him, to see Him, and to give,
Whatever riches that we have, and to serve Him while we live."

"Now that we have seen His face, and satisfied our soul,
We will go back to our homes, in peace that's been made whole."

"We will spend the night with you, resting with you here.
We only want to serve this Child, from us you need not fear."

Joseph smiled and thanked them, giving them his hand,
"I do believe God sent you here. You are welcome in our land."

And so we all went to our rest; I slept a peaceful night.
I felt that God was leading us, and all would come out right.

In the morning when we rose, I saw the others had no rest.
They were tired and worried, wondering what was best.

One man said an angel dream explained what they must do.
They must not return to Herod, but take another way they knew.

"We'll go back to our own land, and we'll leave while it's still light.
We'll travel as quickly as we can, and we will not stop at night".

Joseph looked at Mary, and he glanced at those three men.
"We also have to go," he said. "We are leaving Bethlehem."

"When I lay in bed last night, I did not sleep or dream.
Still I feel uneasy; things aren't always what they seem."

"I can't explain my thoughts and fears. I just know that it is so.
I feel that we must leave this place, that it's time for us to go."

The tallest of the three men, nodded and he smiled,
"You are very wise to do this, you must protect this Child."

"We are well provisioned, with food and drink for days.
Let us share supplies with you, and help you on your way."

"We see you have one small beast, we will make that two.
One to hold your wife and child, and one to carry you."

Mary smiled and thanked him, her eyes were bright with tears.
"Your kindness we'll remember, through all our living years."

"I know that you'll be leaving here before the set of sun.
God will bless you all your days, for the deeds that you have done."

Those three wise men left our inn, with camels and with packs.
We didn't know which way they'd gone, if we were ever asked.

Joseph slept that afternoon; he thought he'd need the rest,
He would trust in God alone, knowing they were blessed.

In dreams, an angel bid him flee and said where they must go.
This last he never spoke aloud, and it was better this was so.

Mary and Joseph and the Child, left at the fall of night,
We watched sadly as they went, till they vanished from our sight.

Later, came a dreadful time, and I thanked the Lord they'd gone,
They were safe and far away, when that awful morning dawned.

Herod's slaughter was grotesque, haunting Bethlehem for years.
Yet we knew our Savior lived, and would someday dry our tears.

"You must have a second birth," He said. "I tell you this is true.
If you aren't born from above, heaven's not for you."

*Jesus answered, Verily, verily, I say unto thee, Except a man be born of
water and of the Spirit, he cannot enter into the kingdom of God.*

John 3:5 KJV

NICODEMUS

I was passing through the temple court when I heard His voice.
A crowd was listening to him without the slightest noise.

I looked and I was puzzled, for I could not recall His name.
His face was flashing in my mind, but no recollection came.

I stood close by and listened, and I liked the things I heard.
They stirred something in my soul, like an echo from God's word.

I knew He was the teacher that came from Galilee.
Why was He so familiar to a Sanhedrin Pharisee?

Work had hardened up His hands, but not His gentle touch.
His face looked used to weather, like it didn't matter much.

I thought about the things He taught, and every word rang true.
I wanted to go and speak with Him, and this desire grew,

I asked a man who was with him, where he spent the night.
Nobody there would tell me, and most likely they were right.

So I sent an errand boy, to "follow where He goes,
Take notice where he makes his camp, then come let me know."

I tried to eat my dinner, but I couldn't concentrate.
The night seemed stopped at early, and I'd go when it was late.

I puzzled and I wondered, where had I seen this man?
Something was familiar, as the back side of my hand.

When at last the hour came, I went into the night.
I hurried toward His camping place, and soon I saw the light.

One young man approached me, and I met his searching eyes.
"I've come to speak with Jesus, His words are always wise."

"Can you take me to Him? I won't be long tonight."
The young man slowly nodded, and led me toward the light.

Jesus came to meet me and He didn't seem surprised.
My name was on His lips, and a smile was in His eyes.

I had my list of questions, but I felt unprepared.
I wondered how to ask them; I wondered if I dared.

I tried to get my thoughts in line, He waited and He smiled.
And somehow in the firelight, His face was like a child.

"I know," I said, "You're sent from God. You are a holy man.
Your teachings and your healing, must be from God's own hand."

"You have sought Me out," He said, " you have come to see.
You study, and you teach the law, and you are asking me."

"You must have a second birth," He said. "I tell you this is true.
If you aren't born from above, heaven's not for you."

I pondered on His statement, and could not understand.
"How can I be born again, when I'm a full grown man?"

"My mother is no longer here, living on this earth.
Even were she here with me, she could not give me birth."

Jesus words were piercing, reaching deep into my soul,
I wanted to be born again, but would this make me whole?

"Flesh is born of flesh," he said, as he looked into my mind,
"And spirit is from spirit, each from its own kind,

Now I you tell in all truth, that new birth from above,
Will set you free and keep you safe, in our Father's love.

Do you ever wonder, as you listen to the wind,
Where on the earth it's going, and even where it's been?

For those who are spirit born, this is how that it must be,
We are guided by the spirit, and the spirit makes us free."

I looked at Him in wonder, for this teaching was not law,
The things that He was saying, were things I never saw.

"How can these things You say to me, possibly be true?
I've studied law all my life, but now I study You?"

Jesus looked so solemn, "You do not see the light.
You are a teacher of the law, and yet you have no sight.

If I tell you earthly things, and these you don't believe,
Can I tell you heavenly things, that you also won't receive?

God gave His son into this world to die for all men's sin.
Just receive His loving gift, and you are not condemned.

God so loved this broken world despite its sin and strife.
Believe on God's only son, and you'll have eternal life.

People love the darkness, and refuse to see God's light.
Anyone who turns away has condemned himself to die."

I talked with Jesus back and forth for at least an hour.
His words were so very new, and yet I felt their power.

And all the time I knew that I had seen this man before!
It was a recollection that I couldn't just ignore.

A LAMB IS BORN

I knew His face, I knew His voice, I'd seen him long ago.
But where on earth I knew Him from, that I didn't know.

"I'm thinking on Your words," I said. "Truth is my only goal."
"I will follow God's own truth to find salvation for my soul."

I recognized His healing touch, and the love that I could see.
Did He possess the power from God to save a Pharisee?

It was then that I remembered where I saw this man before.
He'd walked into the temple through an open door.

Twelve years old, he said he was, when they asked His age.
A peaceful happy boy he seemed, with the wisdom of a sage.

I stood aside and listened while the elders asked His name.
He was plied with questions, and His answers quickly came.

He spoke with a quiet knowing far beyond his years.
He asked and answered questions without a trace of fear.

I had marveled at this boy child who knew far more than me.
His words revealed great knowledge, beyond what I could see!

And then His parents came for Him; His mother was in tears.
They both were sick with worry, in the grip of many fears.

They hurried out with their son, and I faintly heard Him say,
"I must do my Father's business, and I have begun today."

I never saw the boy again, but before me stood the Man.
It all became quite clear to me, with the answer in my hand.

I felt my breath in short hard gasps, I was kneeling on the ground.
This surely was the Son of God, this Man that I had found.

"Lord, I now believe," I said. "All you say is true."
"My eyes are opened and I see. Now I must follow you."

NICODEMUS

I saw for just a moment, that young boy in front of me.
I knew He understood this, and I knew I was set free.

"Go back home," He said to me. "I shall depend on you.
Stay in the temple for a while. You will know what to do."

I turned away, lost in thought, feeling somewhat strange,
Since I found God's Holy One, how would my life be changed?

I left Him at His campsite, and hurried back to town,
Every word He said to me, must now be written down.

These important things, that He made known to me,
Were meant for all the world, not just this Pharisee.

For God so loved this world that He sent His Son to die,
That whosoever believed on Him, would have eternal life.

"Jesus reached for Sarah, and He held her for a while.
He kissed her on her rosy cheek, and she began to smile."

But Jesus said, Suffer little children, and forbid them not, to come unto me: for of such is the kingdom of heaven.

Matthew 19:14 KJV

LOAVES AND FISHES

My little sister, Sarah, has long black curly hair.
She is very pretty, but she needs a lot of care.

I sat beside her bed today to think what I could do.
She was blue around her eyes, and her fingernails were blue.

She is my mother's youngest child, the first since she had me.
I am ten years old now, but our Sarah's only three.

I thought about how weak she was, and had no strength to play,
And then I knew what I must do, and that there was a way!

There was someone who could help, the One I had to see!
I knew that I must find Him, and bring Him home with me.

I'll go to where He's teaching, and I'll be there by noon!
"Mother," I said, "I have got to go! I have to do this soon!"

Mother looked at Sarah, and then she looked at me.
"I can't let you go alone! You're half the world to me."

"You know I love your sister, but between you I can't choose.
Jacob, you're my precious son, I couldn't stand to lose."

"Your father was killed a year ago, by bandits on the road.
I can't have you take this chance, and let you bear this load."

Just then our neighbor, Thomas, came to our front door,
With my best friend, Samuel, in a group with several more.

"We're going now to hear the Teacher, He's not so far away!"
"Mother," I cried, "Let me go too! Please don't make me stay!"

Mother looked at Thomas, her eyes were open wide!
"If I let him go with you, will you keep him by your side?"

Thomas pledged to watch me, saying, "You need have no fright!
We'll bring him back by evening, or at the morning's light."

I saw my mother waver, then I knew she'd let me go.
I saw her glance at Sarah, who couldn't seem to grow.

"Jacob, if I let you go, there are some things that you'll need.
By the time you find the Teacher, you'll want some food to eat."

"I'll pack a lunch for you to take, it will hardly be a minute.
Loaves and fish and a little bag! I'll just put them in it."

"Hurry, hurry," Samuel called. "We need to get there fast!
Everyone is leaving now! We can't be the last!"

She handed me the leather bag. she kissed my nose and eyes.
"Come back soon!" she whispered. "I am praying this is wise."

I kissed my mother and my sister, then I ran out quick.
Very soon I could tell the Teacher, about Sarah being sick.

There were a lot of people, in the crowd ahead of me.
They were talking about the Teacher, and what they hoped to see.

They all were looking for Him, and they hoped he'd make them well,
I prayed that I'd get close to Him; I had so much to tell.

Thomas led us along the path; for two long hours we walked.
I got more and more excited as we all smiled and talked.

Then I saw a gathering, on a hill not far away.
I knew it was the Teacher, and I wondered what He'd say.

We crowded close and settled down, on the grassy hill.
His words were like cool water, and I could drink my fill.

He talked about His Father, and the love He felt for us.
That we must love each other, that we always need to trust.

I knew that I believed Him, and the peace that I could feel.
I loved Him as He spoke to us, and raised His hand to heal.

As the day drew on to evening, I felt my hunger grow;
I thought about the lunch I had, and then I didn't know.

They crowded round the Master, to reach His loving hand.
He must be getting hungry, here in this empty land.

I thought again about the food, I carried in my pack.
I knew it all had come from God, and I must give it back.

A man stood near the Teacher, and I tried to catch his eye.
I thought that I could talk to him, at least I'd better try.

I pushed till I stood next to him, then I touched his sleeve.
"Sir," I said. "Here's something, that I think the Teacher needs",

The man looked down at me, and smiled, "What is it that you've got?"
"Bread and fishes for His dinner, but I haven't got a lot."

"I'll take you to the Master, I'm sure He needs to eat."
And then we walked toward Jesus, through the dust and heat.

I heard the Teacher tell His men, that they must feed the crowd.
I whispered, "That's impossible," but I didn't say it loud.

I knew two fish and five small loaves wasn't much to share.
"That's all we have," my new friend said, "there's no food anywhere."

A LAMB IS BORN

Jesus smiled, put out His hand, and took the leather pack.
The food went in a basket, and His hand was on my back.

"Jacob, you are very kind, to give your food to Me.
My Father now will bless us all, as you are blessing Me."

Jesus lifted up the food, high above His head,
He was looking into heaven, and this was what He said:

"Loving Father, we thank you now, for the food that you provide,
I ask You, please, to bless this meal, as we share it far and wide."

When He brought the basket down, and set it on the ground,
It overflowed with loaves and fish, enough to spread around.

His men served out the bread and fish to all the people there.
I saw that now there was enough for everyone to share.

I heard there were five thousand people, counting just the men.
The scraps had filled twelve baskets, when they picked them up again.

Some were tired and lay right down, to wait for morning light,
And some set off in friendly groups, to make it home that night.

I began to look for Thomas, and for Samuel, my friend.
They were nowhere to be seen, and the day was near it's end.

My mother would be waiting, and worry till the dawn,
I didn't like to think about, all the hours I'd been gone!

I hadn't talked to Jesus, I hadn't made my plea,
I hadn't mentioned Sarah, I had only thought of me.

Jesus' men climbed in their boat, to sail away somewhere.
No one saw the Master go; He simply wasn't there.

I slowly sat down on the grass, and I thought I'd better pray,
Surely God would help me, as I tried to find my way.

After that, I stood and looked, across the crowded land,
Tears were running down my face, then someone took my hand.

"Jacob, let Me walk with you, I'll not leave you here alone."
Jesus' eyes were smiling down, and I knew He'd take me home.

"Oh, yes, please!" I said to Him. "I think I've lost my way.
My mother will be worried, for I've been gone all day."

"I can't find Thomas and my friend, and that's where I need to be",
"I spoke to Thomas," Jesus said, "He knows you're safe with me."

We walked together down the hill, the grass was wet with dew,
He seemed to take away my fears, made everything brand new.

I started then to tell him how my father died,
And all about my sister, and how my mother cried.

He held my hand and listened, and I just talked and talked,
In a while, I noticed, how quickly we had walked.

I saw our house in front of me, my mother at the gate.
I knew that she'd been waiting there, though it was getting late.

"Sarah will get better now," I told her with a grin!
"I have brought the Teacher, and you must ask Him in!"

"Take Him in to Sarah, where she is lying down,
And tomorrow she'll get up and be running all around!."

Mother hurried to the house, and opened up the door.
I saw her go to Sarah, and she scooped her off the floor!

"Look!" she cried. "Sarah's well! You see how her skin glows!"
"She was healed this afternoon! She's pink down to her toes."

"I thank you, Lord, for healing her, before my very eyes!"
Mother now was kneeling down, smiling as she cried.

"Get up," He said, "Your child is well, your love is very great."
And even through your hardest times, you have kept your faith."

Jesus reached for Sarah, and He held her for a while.
He kissed her on her rosy cheek, and she began to smile.

He handed her to Mother, and bid us both good-night.
I could see it made Him happy, that our lives had been set right.

I wanted just to thank Him, to tell Him so much more,
But somehow right in front of us, He'd gone out the door.

"Jacob, He's saved your sister from a certain death.
My son, we're called to serve Him till our final breath."

"Mother, He's the son of God. I know now this is true.
We must tell the whole wide world, the things that God can do!"

"God will surely care for us like the lilies in the field.
He will see our sickness, and make sure that we are healed!"

"We don't ever have to worry about an empty dish!
Jesus fed five thousand men with our loaves and fish."

"I stretched out my hand to Him, thanking God I'd made it here.
A tide of light rushed through me, and God felt very near!"

And a woman having an issue of blood twelve years, which had spent all her living upon physicians, neither could be healed of any, 44 Came behind him, and touched the border of his garment: and immediately her issue of blood stanched.

Luke 8:43,44 KJV

PUT ASIDE

Jonas pledged to love me when he chose me as his bride.
When I became "untouchable" I was cast aside.

We had a happy marriage and a baby that first year.
With the three of us together, I hardly shed a tear.

A second, third, and fourth child, then my body changed.
It seemed I always was "unclean", I was always fighting pain.

It didn't happen quickly, but so slow I hardly knew.
I know of other women who have lived this story too.

I couldn't do the cooking because I was "unclean".
I couldn't mind the children; I hardly dared be seen.

The law was very clear on the things I could not do.
Jonas tried to help me cope, but he had his problems too.

I suffered more than I could say with a constant bloody flow.
The pain got more and more intense, but Jonas didn't know.

I felt Jonas' growing fear. "Will you always be like this?"
"God will heal me soon," I said. This was my deepest wish.

My painful curse now ruled my life, and ruined every day.
Synagogue was forbidden me, so I couldn't even pray.

Jonas had enough one day, said he had a life to live.
The care our children needed was more than he could give.

The law would grant him a release, a writing of divorce.
He must have a helpmate, and it wasn't me of course.

The day he bade me leave the house, he looked so very pained.
But a brand new wife was waiting, and his love for me had waned.

I had saved some money back; I was a careful wife.
It wasn't much and I knew well, it wouldn't last my life.

I slowly walked across the town, to my brother's home.
I hoped that he would take me in, or I'd be left to roam.

My brother seemed quite willing to let me earn my keep.
He had a little shed where he said that I could sleep.

He said that I could help his wife, if my sickness should abate.
He said that they would bring me food when the family ate.

So I settled in the shed, and there I've lived for years.
I grew weak and hopeless as I lived out my worst fears.

All the money that I brought, I've spent to find a cure.
Nothing helped, the money's gone, of that at least I'm sure.

Those four babies that I bore; they all were lost to me.
I lived to love and pray for, those babes my heart could see.

I lived there with a leaky roof. I lived there in the cold.
I lived there while I watched, and felt my body growing old.

My brother tried to help me. He fixed the leaky room.
His wife brought me more blankets, to warm my living tomb.

I used to think the synagogue was the only place for prayer,
But in that little shed I found that God is everywhere.

PUT ASIDE

Jonas, with our oldest child, walked past my shed one day.
Jonas wouldn't let her talk, he made her come away.

Naomi was my first born babe, and she was nearly grown,
Soon enough she'd marry, and have children of her own.

The next day my Naomi came past the shed once more.
She walked right up and talked to me, through the open door.

I walked out, one day in spring, when I felt a little stronger.
The sun soon warmed my shaking limbs, so I walked a little longer.

Nearby a man was speaking, to a crowd all gathered round.
His voice was clear and I didn't hear, any other sound.

He talked about divorcement, men who set their wives apart.
Why should a woman suffer, from her husband's hardened heart ?

I thought that He must know me, for my soul had heard his voice.
I thought that His kind words might give me reason to rejoice.

I went back home to my little shed, and found some dinner there.
My brother's wife was kind and good, and of a mind to share.

I had grown to love her, my brother's gentle wife.
Each day she encouraged me, to hold on to my life.

I fell asleep that night again, lying on the floor.
Yet in my soul, as I slept, I began to hope once more.

I woke early in the morning with weak and painful limbs,
And when I stood up on my feet, the room began to spin.

My brother's wife was speaking, her face was all aglow.
"There's a man and He can help. That's where you need to go!"

She said this man called Jesus, was healing all who came!
"You must go and see Him! He can end your shame."

I couldn't see how this could be, without committing sin.
How could He ever heal me, if He couldn't touch my skin?

I prayed to God a desperate prayer, as I tottered down the lane,
'Please help me to get close enough, so He can end this pain'.

I knew He couldn't touch me, still God showed me a way.
I would touch the knotted hem of the shawl He wore to pray.

Soon I saw Him, in a crowd , right in front of me,
Talking to a wealthy man, beneath a shady tree.

People milled around Him, each trying to be heard,
But Jesus was just listening, to this man's every word.

I went carefully, through the crowd, hoping no one saw.
If I touched a person, they would know I broke the law.

I may have brushed some people, as I pushed my way past them,
I didn't notice anyone, while I was looking for his hem.

Before me stood a holy Man, keeping Moses every law.
I knew He was a man of God, without a single flaw.

If I could touch His garment's hem, I knew I would be healed.
I understood the power that this holy Man could wield.

I stretched out my hand to Him, thanking God I'd made it here.
A tide of light rushed through me, and God felt very near!

Then the light had passed away, and I lay on the ground.
The Rabbi spoke out loudly, as He turned and looked around.

"Who touched me?" He was asking. It was clear to me He knew.
"You're in a crowd!" someone said. "They all are touching You."

"Someone touched Me," He insisted. "I felt the power go!
Someone here received it, and they must tell me so!"

I crawled to Him on my knees, I was crouching on the ground.
"Sir, I touched your hem." I said. I kept my head bowed down.

"I've been unclean for many years; I've had no peace or rest.
There has been no help for me. Now, I have nothing left."

"This morning I could barely stand. My pain was like a knife."
But when my fingers touched Your hem, I was filled with life."

He slowly smiled, then reached down, and took my shaking hand.
He raised me up, and steadied me, as though this were His plan.

"Your faith has healed you, Daughter, You are now made whole."
Now go and lead a normal life. Health is in your soul."

He turned back, to the waiting man, and they quickly walked away.
But I could see His smiling eyes. and they're with me to this day.

My brother's wife was waiting, and I loved her beaming face.
Her arms were warm around me, in a long delayed embrace.

She led me to the mikveh where I could bathe and dress.
The clothing that she gave me must have been her best.

She said, "Our children need your help, they love you as I do,
And if your own can come to us, they are welcome too."

"I think you'll see Naomi soon," she told me with a smile.
"She comes to us when she can, and she longs to stay a while."

"Now, she can bring the younger ones; they still remember you,
Jonas' wife has cared for them, but she has children too."

"Naomi is her mother's child, she's never stopped believing,
That you would once again be well. She suffered from your leaving."

I'd forgiven Jonas, many years ago,
I sent a message to him, just to tell him so.

God and the Rabbi healed me, completely changed my life.
I've healthy years in front of me with my brother and his wife.

I want to know the Rabbi, I want to hear him talk.
I want to listen to His voice, and follow where He walks.

I know that He's a man of God; they say He's God's own son,
And He will be my guiding light until my life is done.

"I walked up to the offering box, the collection for the poor.
I put my pennies in it, and I knelt there on the floor."

And he saw also a certain poor widow casting in thither two mites.
3 And he said, Of a truth I say unto you, that this poor widow
hath cast in more than they all:
4 For all these have of their abundance cast in unto the offerings of
God: but she of her penury hath cast in all the living that she had.

Luke 1:2-4 KJV

THE WIDOW'S COINS

When I arose that morning, there was nothing left.
I wondered if my children would slowly starve to death.

Nothing in the cupboard, no food for them to eat,
No coins were in my pocket, no shoes for their young feet.

Three children soon would come to me, asking to be fed.
I could give them nothing, no oil or fish or bread.

I couldn't think what I could do; I'd led a sheltered life.
I knew how to run a household as a mother and a wife.

Maybe I could learn to serve, working in a house of wealth.
I felt so very thankful that I still was in good health.

Benjamin turned five that day, and I had nothing left to sell.
All the worries in my heart were things I couldn't tell.

I went to wake up Rachel as soon as it was day.
She could watch her brothers while I was away.

"I'm going to the temple," I told her with a smile.
"I'll be coming back with food in just a little while."

"Mother, you're not going to beg!" Her voice was horrified.
"I promise you I won't do that!" I prayed I hadn't lied.

A LAMB IS BORN

I thought that I might meet a friend who'd stop and say, "hello".
Maybe they would offer help to someone they used to know.

It was all so different when Isaac still was living.
But Isaac died, and now our friends had their fill of giving.

Isaac left us money, and the house where we could dwell.
We were very careful, we sold what we could sell.

For a while I ran the business, I worked and carried on;
But Isaac was a builder, and his building hands were gone.

Soon we'd have to sell our house; that would leave us on the street.
But we had to have the money if we were going to eat.

I hugged Rachel, then I left, before the boys could see.
Sometimes the market people would give old food to me.

This morning there was nothing, nothing I could find,
Nothing I could take back home; "nothing" filled my mind.

I turned and left the market, meeting no ones eyes.
Former friends all looked away, and this was no surprise.

Next there was the temple, where I could make my prayer.
If I had an offering, I could leave it there.

I'd given prayers and offerings till I could give no more,
And still there was no answer, and we were no less poor.

My eyes were blurring as I walked quickly down the street,
And then I saw a miracle, just lying by my feet.

Two small coins were lying there, tarnished and quite brown.
To me they looked like heaven; they could turn my day around!

I scooped them up and clutched them, dirty though they were!
These could buy some breakfast, that I knew for sure.

THE WIDOW'S COINS

I hurried to the temple, praises filled my mind!
I made a vow, that for now, my worries were behind.

I came into the outer court, saw the beggars sitting there;
The lame and blind and helpless with not a soul to care.

My heart was filled with sorrow, and my eyes were filled with tears.
These people sat there every day, some of them for years.

I had a healthy body, with healthy children, too.
I felt sure that God would show us, something we could do.

I felt the pennies in my hand. I clutched them to my heart!
I didn't want to give them up, but I had to do my part.

The priests were in the temple, and scribes in their fine dress.
They seemed to look at me with scorn; still I must do my best.

A man that once hired Isaac threw in coins that looked like gold.
Did I need to give my coins, so dirty and so old?

I walked up to the offering box, the collection for the poor.
I put my pennies in it, and I knelt there on the floor.

"Lord," I said, "It's all I have; But I have learned and taken heed.
Please use these coins to help someone who has a greater need."

I thought I heard someone laugh, a snicker or a scoff.
Did one scribe say "so little", then cover with a cough?

Then I heard another voice, and every word was clear.
"This widow gave in sacrifice, her coins were very dear."

"This man gave from his great wealth, following the law.
The widow's given all she has; she gave the most of all."

I tell you now to love your God, with all your mind and soul and heart.
The things you need will come to you, for God will do His part.

I saw it was the Teacher, the One we loved to hear.
I thought I'd stay and listen, for I was longing to be near.

When He left, He passed close by, He smiled and I felt blessed.
"Your load is heavy," He said to me, "but God will give you rest."

I left the temple full of hope, not knowing how we'd live.
But maybe I'd learned something, about the need to give.

It was time to go back home, and I had no food to bring,
Yet somewhere in my soul I found a song that I could sing.

Then someone came and joined me as I walked along.
It was an unfamiliar man, and he looked both broad and strong.

I glanced at him and looked away. Why was he by my side?
I didn't think I knew him, yet he stayed there, stride for stride.

"Excuse me, Ma'am," he finally said. "I think you are Isaac's bride.
If I'm wrong, forgive me, and at least I'll know I tried."

"Yes," I said, "He married me, though fifteen years have passed."
And now I am his widow, all this year and the last."

He smiled at this, a gentle smile, and it nestled in my mind.
Then he began to talk to me, and his voice was very kind.

"My home has been in Ephesus. For years I've lived alone.
Then I heard my brother died, and so I have come home."

That man there in the temple, who put in coins of gold--
He used to buy his goods from me, when he wasn't very old.

I've met him when he travels, he goes as far as Rome,
So I went to visit him when I got back home.

We walked together to the temple, to offer and to pray,
And there we saw you coming in so early in the day.

He spoke then of my brother, for I told him Isaac died.
He wasn't sure, but he thought, that you were Isaac's bride."

I turned and stared at this man and I had to hide my tears.
Isaac had an older brother, that he hadn't seen in years.

"You came too late," I softly said, "I want you just to know."
"He often spoke of you to me. He really loved you so!"

"Please forgive me, Lady, that I didn't come in time.
I have no wife or children, no family that is mine."

"In law, I must support Isaac's children and his wife,
I think that there's no better way, than this to spend my life."

"Are there children, Lady? And are you feeling need?
I truly want to help you if there are children you must feed."

I stared at him, my eyes were wide. Was he meaning what he said?
"Three," I said, "and yes, we are. In our cupboard there's no bread."

"Please," he said, "Take me along, I want to meet those three.
They are my brother's children, and my only family."

Benjamin was by the door, waiting when we came,
"You look like my father--alike but not the same,"

I said, "This is your father's brother, He's your uncle Saul.
He has asked a friend to go, and bring breakfast for us all."

Benjamin had guessed the truth, the truth I hadn't seen.
My head felt fuzzy and unreal, like I was in a dream.

Jude and Rachel were more shy, hung back a little while.
They came to him when they saw he had their father's smile.

I spent the day in wonder that our lives had turned around.
In the twinkling of an eye, the lost had now been found.

As I went to sleep that night, I thought I'd passed a test.
Seek first your Father's kingdom, and He will add the rest.

That Man there in the temple, the One that we both heard;
Saul thinks that He was sent from God! He is the living Word.

I'll go with Saul and seek Him out, hear all He has to say.
Where He leads, we shall follow and we will find the way.

"Soldiers come and soldiers go, according to my word,
Yet before You I am nothing, Don't come in, my Lord."

*6 Then Jesus went with them. And when he was now not far from the
house, the centurion sent friends to him, saying unto him, Lord, trouble
not thyself: for I am not worthy that thou shouldest enter under my roof:*

Luke 7:6 KJV

THE CENTURION'S SERVANT BOY

Luke 7:1-10

I arose at four today, with a lot of work to do.
All the things I needed done, my servant surely knew.

The house was cold and quiet, the fire had long gone out.
The servant boy must be asleep, so I gave a shout.

I expected to see Jonah, scrambling out of bed,
Hurrying to help me, not needing to be led.

I waited for a moment-- something here was wrong,
Jonah loved to be up first; he never slept too long!

I went into the kitchen, to check the fire keep.
I saw him wrapped in blankets, shaking in his sleep.

Kneeling down, I touched his burning, fevered face.
He seemed totally withdrawn from this time and place.

He might as well be wandering in some far off land.
He muttered words now and then I couldn't understand.

"Jonah," I said softly, pushing back his hair.
"Jonah, what's the matter? Jonah, are you there?"

Jonah didn't answer, except a hurting little cry.
I suddenly was full of fear that this boy might die!

I drew a bowl of water, to cool his hands and face,
Then I started up the fire to warm his sleeping place.

I woke up the household, for this boy needed care.
Hot drinks and poultices could be brought to bear.

I told the cook to heat some broth, and try to make him drink.
All the household loved the boy, and we'd figure out this thing.

I'm a Roman soldier, I'm here to keep the peace.
Jonah is my errand boy, and like a son to me.

Jonah now is nearly twelve, a smiling happy boy.
I brought him here to my home, and he has brought us joy.

Jonah was an orphan child, surviving in this town,
He seemed to have no family left, that anyone had found.

I like the Jewish people here; they respect the law.
I helped them build a synagogue, the best they ever saw.

I've lived here with these people; now their God is my Lord.
I can't worship in their temple, but I can listen to His word.

I've built my house, I've hired my staff, things are going well.
And now my Jonah's fallen ill, who can ever tell?

My cook, whose name is Martha, came to let me know--
The trip that I was planning, it's better not to go.

I had a look at Jonah, still lying sick and white;
There had to be a way, somehow, to set this matter right.

I am a Roman officer with money and with power,
And yet my little errand boy is dying by the hour.

I thought about this Jesus; He goes throughout this land.
If there were a way to reach Him, He has a healing hand.

THE CENTURION'S SERVANT BOY

Still I am a Roman, and He's a rabbi healing Jews,
They don't really trust me, and I understand their views.

I spoke again to Martha, she was blinking back her tears.
She thinks that Jonah's dying, and I frankly share her fears.

"Martha, get your husband," I said to her at last.
"You've got to go get Reuben, and you must bring him fast."

Soon Reuben stood before me. I said, " Jonah's death is near,
You have to go to Jesus, and the message must be clear."

"Please take another elder from your house of prayer,
Both of you must go to Him. You must meet Him there.

You will ride my fastest horses, I'll tell you what to say,
I'll send my letters with you, but I'll stay here and pray.

This teacher is nearby, He can't be far away,
I know that He was teaching near here yesterday."

I set the men on horseback, with letters to this Man.
Then I went to stay with Jonah, and I sat with folded hands.

I thought that it was right to kneel, and ask the Jewish God for aid.
Jonah was a Jewish boy, and I believed the prayer I prayed.

Rabbi Jesus is a man who tells people what to do.
If He wants to heal this boy, then he will make it through.

I longed so much to go myself, but I am of no worth.
I am just a Roman, and His God owns the earth.

I sat with Jonah and I prayed, I held him in my arms,
"Please, Lord, don't let this precious boy, come to any harm."

Jonah lay there in his bed, with eyes that had no sight,
And I just sat there praying that God would make it right.

I sat at least two hours there, and I could see no change.
I was still in constant prayer and Jonah looked the same.

Through the open window, sounds fell on my ear,
Even through the distance, the words seemed pretty clear.

I saw the Master coming; soon He'd be beneath my roof,
And yet I was not worthy. He had to know the truth.

He must understand my plight, He must know my gentile state.
He must not come into my house, nor even pass the gate.

I am a Roman soldier, commanding many men.
I sent my servant to tell Him "Please do not come in,

Soldiers come and soldiers go, according to my word,
Yet before You I am nothing, Don't come in, my Lord.

My servant boy lies dying; be assured that this is true,
I know Jonah will recover, with just one word from You."

My servant spoke these words to Him, I could hear his voice.
I knew he told Him everything, according to my choice.

Then I heard the Master speak, talking to a crowd.
I saw their amazement, at the words He spoke aloud.

I couldn't hear all that He said, but I understood His tone.
He would do as I had begged, and leave me here alone.

I couldn't see His smiling lips, but I felt His smiling face.
I saw Him lift His hand to me, as He turned to walk away.

Soon Reuben and the elder came, and asked to speak to me.
"Jesus says that Jonah's healed, your heart can be set free".

Jesus said there's one thing that He needs to tell,
He hasn't seen faith this great, in all of Israel.

THE CENTURION'S SERVANT BOY

I looked up to see a happy child; our Jonah standing there,
I threw my arms around the boy, forgetting all my care.

Jonah looked to me as though he had slept in perfect health,
A look you couldn't purchase, with any kind of wealth!

Then I looked at Reuben, and the elder at his side.
Both of them were smiling, but as for me, I cried.

Reuben's eyes were shining, Martha was in tears.
All of us loved Jonah, and would for many years.

We all loved this Jesus; God's own precious son,
I knew He would unite us; Jew and Gentile could be one.

"Teacher," I called out to Him, my voice was near a shout.
"My daughter has a demon, and you can cast it out!"

*26 The woman was a Greek, a Syrophenician by nation; and she
besought him that he would cast forth the devil out of her daughter.*

Mark 7:26 KJV

PUPPY'S CRUMBS

Mark 7:24-30

My daughter's nine years old now, and I've nearly lost my mind.
Priscilla occupies my thoughts, her care takes all my time.

She was her father's special pet, but lately she has changed.
She is another person now, our lives can't be the same.

She will seem to be far away; sometimes she cries for hours.
Sometimes, she doesn't know us; she has rages, then she cowers.

We see her fall down on the ground, gripped by awful fears,
Writhing about, and crying out, with contorted face and tears.

She fell into the fire last night; her hands was badly burned.
I tried to put some ointment on, the way that I had learned.

Priscilla was so very strong, her father couldn't hold her.
She wouldn't let me near her hands; it did no good to scold her.

The neighbors point and whisper, and avoid us all around.
We are hurt, and we are hopeless, for help cannot be found.

We live for our Priscilla, we dream that she'll be well,
That she'll get up one morning and walk right out of hell.

My sister came to visit me; that was yesterday.
She said Priscilla is possessed, and that we need to pray.

"We've gone to all the gods we know, with prayer and sacrifice.
We've given to them on and on, and never asked the price."

My sister said there's someone! He goes throughout the land,
He heals whoever comes to Him, and seeks His helping hand.

"He came here yesterday", she said, for she saw Him on the road.
She thought that He looked weary, as though He bore a load.

"He likely came out here to spend a restful quiet day.
You must go and speak to Him before He goes away."

"One thing to remember, He's a rabbi healing Jews,
But He has cast out demons, so what have you to lose?"

I told her that our neighbor Jews, say that we're 'unclean',
I thought all people were the same; I don't know what they mean.

Their way of life is rather strange, but they strive to keep their law.
And when they sin, they are sorry, in a way I never saw.

We've never served the Jewish God, we're foreigners and Greeks.
But if He will heal Priscilla, I will worship on my knees!

"Prisca, you must go," she said, "and tell Him what you need!
Explain about Priscilla, and then you beg and plead".

It really seemed my sister had reasoned this out right.
In the darkness of my nightmare life, I began to see a light!

"Prisca," she said to me again, "This is really real!
I have watched Him closely, and He can touch and heal".

"The lame have walked, the deaf can hear, the blind can even see!
You must not wait! Just go ahead, and leave the girl with me."

I heard Priscilla start to scream, and I almost didn't go.
Could my sister manage her? I really didn't know.

"Prisca, go!" my sister cried. "Go while I am here"
And so I ran out from my house, choking down my fear.

I knew about the man she saw. I'd heard Him talked about.
This was just a little town, and I could seek Him out.

I found Him talking to a crowd. His disciples stood between.
They were trying to protect Him, but I was going to be seen.

I pushed my way into their midst, to get up close to Him,
He would have to hear my plea, if it cost me life or limb.

"Sir," I called as I got close. "Sir, I must talk to you!"
He paid me no attention, so I kept on pushing through.

"Teacher," I called out to Him, my voice was near a shout.
"My daughter has a demon, and you can cast it out!"

"Rabbi, You must hear me. She needs your help right now!"
I found myself in front of Him, I wasn't sure quite how.

"I came," He said, "for Israel. I see that you're a Greek.
What have I to do with you? What is it that you seek?"

"I'm not sent to feed wild dogs. The children need my care."
His words were hurting to my heart, but I couldn't leave it there.

"Sir," I said to Him once more, lifting up my eyes,
"If You could see my daughter, you would listen to her cries."

"I am desperate for Priscilla. A demon has her soul.
Please bring her out of bondage. You can make her whole.

You say you're sent to feed the children, meaning just the Jews.
My daughter's need is very great, why can't you heal her too?"

"Snarling dogs are not deserving, first let your people come,
But a pup beneath the table, is not kept from eating crumbs.

Children can be messy eaters, so food falls on the floor,
This can feed a hungry puppy, while the child is given more."

I feared that I had said too much, that He'd make me go away,
But His smiling face before me, was like sunshine on my day.

"Woman, this wise saying, speaks very well of you.
Your child is healed. Go home and look. You will see it's true."

I felt dazed and yet believing, I fell down on my knees.
"Sir, I thank you from my heart. You have set my daughter free."

I hurried home to see Priscilla. Was she herself once more?.
She was sleeping on her couch; I could see her from the door.

I knelt beside my sleeping child, she seemed so full of peace.
Her childish hand, without a burn, lay beside her rosy cheek.

In sleep she smiled, and snuggled down, her body deep in rest.
This wasn't just a puppy's crumb, He'd given her His best!

Later, when she wakened, she hugged her father tight,
and whispered she no longer feared the demons in the night.

I cooked and made a joyous feast for all of us to share.
We stumbled and repeated a new and thankful prayer.

This was a prayer my sister knew, one she heard Him say,
Thanking God for His love, for our food, and for this day.

"Prisca, dear," my husband said, "What a wonder you have done!"
"No," I said, "it wasn't me. This came from God's own son."

"I saw he loves His fellow Jews; I know now He loves the Greek.
His love is there for all of us, if we truly seek.

Both Jew and Greek will follow Him, more will come each day.
Like us, they'll know that He alone, can show the world the way.

"I had no linen with me, to massage and soothe His skin;
And so I used my unbound hair, till His feet were dry again."

3 Then took Mary a pound of ointment of spikenard, very costly, and anointed the feet of Jesus, and wiped his feet with her hair: and the house was filled with the odour of the ointment.

John 12:3 KJV

MARY'S PERFUME

My brother came home early; he said he wasn't feeling well.
His pallid face and shaking hands, rang a warning bell.

Martha brought her healing draught, and sat by him till he slept.
By then he looked so very ill, I turned away and wept.

He was worse by morning's light, and our hearts were cold with fear.
He didn't eat, he didn't drink, he seemed not to see or hear.

I stared at my sister, Martha, and she gazed right back at me.
There must be something we could do, but what I couldn't see.

"We've got to get a doctor or Lazarus will die!,"
Martha's voice was frantic. "But is there one close by?"

"Martha, send for Jesus! We've heard all the things he's done.
He also loves our brother! He'll turn this way and come."

Fear and worry seemed to ease, and she rubbed away a tear.
"I'll send our servant on a horse, that will bring the Master here."

The servant rode away to search, within that very hour,
We knew he'd bring the Master back with all His healing power.

We went back to sit with Lazarus, we bathed his fevered skin,
We tried to give him comfort, in a fight we couldn't win.

A LAMB IS BORN

We knew that Jesus had to come, or Lazarus would die,
If Martha's potions couldn't save him, still she had to try.

We waited though the afternoon, we waited through the night.
Lazarus grew weaker still, and passed at the morning's light.

Still we waited there for Jesus, we knew His healing gift!
If He could only touch our brother, Lazarus would yet live.

But Jesus didn't come to us, no matter how we prayed.
So we opened up the tomb where our brother would be laid.

Lazarus was buried there and we were left to grieve,
Jesus hadn't come at all, so there was no reprieve.

Our servant soon returned, but without our Friend and Lord.
He said he spoke with Jesus, but he got no healing word.

The house was filled with weeping, with family and friends.
Still nothing came from Jesus, not a message did He send.

Martha's soul was hurting; if his life could not be saved,
Jesus should come at least and mourn at Lazarus' grave.

Four days passed in sadness, friends came to us and went.
But there was no sign of Jesus, just weeping and lament.

How well I could remember sitting by the Master's feet.
Martha looked at me and beckoned, but I wouldn't yield my seat.

She demanded Jesus tell me, that I must help her serve the guests,
He smiled and scolded Martha, saying my choice was the best.

Martha quickly finished her serving and her chores,
Then she came and joined me, with a cushion on the floor.

We listened to His teaching. We loved everything He said.
Our hearts were quick to follow anywhere He led.

MARY'S PERFUME

He often came to visit, with His disciples and His mother,
I was sure He loved us all; His best friend was my brother.

Now Lazarus was gone from us, our dear Friend never came.
Just one word from Jesus, and all would have stayed the same.

Suddenly we heard a cry; they saw Him near the city gate!
At last our Lord would be here, but His coming was too late.

My sister ran to meet Him, to tell Him all the things she thought.
I just stayed there with my friends, my trust in Him seemed lost.

Soon Martha came and told me, that now I had to go;
Our Lord was there to tell me, some things I need to know.

I hurried to where He waited, I ran for near a mile,
I knew He couldn't ease my grief, could not even make me smile.

When I finally came to Jesus, I fell exhausted at His feet.
My face was soaked with sweat and tears; I could hardly speak.

"Lord," I gasped, "We needed you, and yet you never came!
You could have made my brother well, and now it's all in vain!"

"Lazarus is in his grave. He died four days ago,
If You had only been here, this would not be so."

"I grieve that you are weeping--both you and your friends.
Show me where you've laid him and all of this can end."

I looked up at the Master, and saw the tears He wept,
I got to my feet and led Him to where my brother slept.

Martha came and joined us, and our relatives and friends.
Jesus came to mourn our brother, and his unexpected end.

I heard some quiet whispers, asking why He had not healed,
His friend and our dear brother, before the tomb was sealed.

Jesus kept looking at the cave, I expected cries and moans,
He looked around at us and said, "Roll away the stone."

I heard my sister's little gasp, "Lord, he's rested there four days!
There will be an awful smell! His body is in decay!"

"Martha, I've explained to you, if you will just believe,
God's glory will be shown here, for all of you to see"

The men went to move the stone, and He began to pray,
"Father, I know You always hear all the words I say.

Father, I say this now, that the people gathered here,
May know that You have sent Me and that You're always near."

He looked up at the open tomb. His voice was near a shout,
"Lazarus," He called His friend, "Lazarus, come out!"

We could see my brother's form, bound head to toe in cloth,
Trying as left the tomb, to get those bindings off.

"Take the linen off his face. Let him breathe and see."
Jesus voice directed us, as we worked to set him free.

Lazarus was alive again, our brother was restored.
But in my heart I'd doubted Him, my Savior and my Lord.

My doubting heart had hurt Him, and yet He could forgive!
He still loved the three of us, and He let our brother live.

He said He was the Way, the Truth, the very Bread of Life.
He said I must forget the doubts, that had cut me like a knife.

My sister's planned a dinner to celebrate our Lord,
She's prepared His favorite dishes, the best we can afford.

My brother has invited, all his friends to come and eat,
And rejoice with the Savior, they all at last will meet.

MARY'S PERFUME

And I'm just the "little sister", and what have I to give?
How can I ever thank Him that He let my brother live?

The only thing I have is this jar of rich perfume.
I could use it in my hair, and let it scent the room.

I thought this was a good thing, then I knew it wouldn't do.
He deserved the perfume. I'm a sinner through and through.

And so I crept into the room where Martha served the men.
The jar of Nard was in my hand, and I was ready to begin.

I anointed first His head, then His painful calloused feet.
The cooling salve would take away, the soreness and the heat.

I had no linen with me, to massage and soothe His skin;
And so I used my unbound hair, till His feet were dry again.

I hoped that I had pleased Him, that some comfort came from me.
My thankful and my contrite heart, was there for Him to see.

One of His disciples, seemed offended to his core!
He said that I should sell the Nard, then go and feed the poor.

"The poor are with you always," we heard our Savior say,
"Very soon I'll be gone, but I'm here with you today."

"Mary, with her ointment, has prepared me for my tomb.
There is not a better use, for Mary's sweet perfume."

We found it was not Lazarus, that God would take away.
Within a week, we all knew, what He meant that day.

And when we heard that He was dead, and lying in a tomb;
We three knew, that He still lived, and would arise quite soon.

"His tomb is empty! He's not there," Her voice was like a song.
"He stood alive before my eyes! I know that I'm not wrong!"

9 Now when Jesus was risen early the first day of the week, he appeared first to Mary Magdalene, out of whom he had cast seven devils.

Mark 16:9 KJV

MY NAME IS MARK

My name is Mark, I was fifteen years, I had grown to be a man.
My mind was set to follow Jesus; and I had made a plan.

I saw Him in the temple, watched Him throw the tables down.
Surely they would make Him king! Soon he'd have a crown!

We all loved John and Peter when they came to use our room.
They told us that their Master would be coming to us soon.

He was coming to our own house where He would eat the feast.
I asked to help my mother serve, so I could talk to Him at least.

We welcomed Jesus and His men as they came and climbed the stair.
We then prepared to bring the food once they were settled there.

We heard their quiet murmurs, as they greeted one another.
Soon enough I caught the smile, and the nod that came from mother.

Going in, I saw a scene that I couldn't understand--
Jesus, kneeling on the floor, with Peter's foot in hand.

The Master, with a towel and bowl, was washing all their feet!
Why would He do this servant's job? He should recline and eat!

"You're not ever washing mine!" Peter cried, dismayed.
"If I don't, you're not my own," Jesus was not swayed.

"You call me 'Master,' and I am, and these things I say are true.
From now on, you must serve each other, just as I am serving you".

He loved them so, and He loved me. I could see it in His eyes.
There wasn't such great love in them--in one I saw surprise!

We went away, left them alone, to eat and talk and share.
I wished that I could listen, sit down and join them there!

Sometime in the evening, one of them came down.
He hurried out into the night, and hardly made a sound.

We cleared the dishes after that; saw they'd shared some wine and bread.
The Master's voice was low and kind; the rest had bowed their heads.

Their room was clean, my work was done, I thought they'd spend the night.
I was tired and sought my bed, tomorrow was in sight.

Before I slept, I heard them coming softly down the stairs.
I recognized His quiet voice; His words came out like prayers.

I only caught a word or two, and I longed to hear much more,
So I draped my sheet around me, and I hurried out the door.

When He saw me next to Peter, He didn't seem surprised,
And I saw an awful sadness, when I looked into His eyes.

We walked across the valley and up a rocky hill,
Into a grove of olives trees, old and very still.

Some of them stayed back a ways, but some with Him went on.
Those He asked to pray with Him were Peter, James and John.

He went still further by Himself, with such a troubled face;
I wondered why He was so sad, in such a peaceful place?

I saw Him slowly kneeling down, I heard His pain-filled cry,
I saw His grim tormented face, as He gazed up at the sky.

The three he left began to pray just as they'd been told.
They huddled close together, for the night was growing cold.

Their eyes were closed; they seemed to fall into a heavy sleep.
I was sad they would betray the watch He'd bid them keep.

Seeing this, He came to them, saying, "Can't you pray one hour?"
"I need your prayers to strengthen me; I'll soon be in their power."

He left them there, then He came back, saying "Please! wake up and pray!
Lest you give into temptation, as you face this fearful day."

Once more He went to pray alone; once more they closed their eyes.
His tortured voice was in my ears, I heard His pleading cries.

His agony continued, anguished and alone.
Drops of blood ran down His face; His voice was just a moan.

"Please, Father, take, this cup away," came through His gritted teeth.
"Don't make me drink this poison; please, let me be released?"

"It's not my will to do this, but Your will must be done."
"Please, give me all the strength I need, and let our wills be one."

Someone came to comfort Him, someone I didn't know;
It might have been an angel, for I thought there was a glow.

He walked back to His sleeping men, for the time to sleep was gone.
"My betrayer comes, get up, let's go!" His voice was hard and strong.

Through the olive trees I heard, a sound like marching feet.
Temple guards surrounded us, leaving no retreat.

I saw the man who left the feast walking in their midst.
He came close to greet his Master with a shameful kiss.

The disciples stood by Jesus, and they gathered close and tight,
They were ready to protect Him, till He put this matter right.

Jesus stood without a sound. He met the leader's eyes.
"Who is it that you seek?" He asked, watching their surprise.

"We want the man called Jesus. We know that He is here."
"I Am He," the Master said, and His words were very clear.

A sudden wind, and His captors fell, flat down in their place.
They lay there dazed and looking up, at the Master's weary face.

Then up they leaped, with angry words, covering up their fear.
Peter yelled, jerked out his sword, and sliced off one man's ear.

I was sure there'd be a battle, sure that He would win,
But Jesus stood there waiting, for what must now begin.

He stretched out His gentle hand, to touch and heal the ear,
And then He looked at Peter, and I had to strain to hear.

"If you live by the sword, so also will you die."
" And what is written, must be done," Jesus held his eye.

The guards all gathered round Him, tying back His hands.
The pushed Him forward roughly, shouting their demands!

His disciples ran away from Him, dodging here and there,
To keep from being dragged along. For Him they took no care.

One temple guard was watching me, and then He grabbed my clothes!
I left my sheet there in his hands, and left Jesus to His foes.

I raced toward home to hide myself, my being filled with shame,
For I was naked to my skin. I'd disgraced my family's name.

Just like the others I had run, mastered by my fears.
Inside my room, I hid alone, and wept unmanly tears.

Peter came into the house and went to the upper room.
I ran upstairs to hear the news, but he was filled with gloom.

MY NAME IS MARK

He sat there in the corner, his hands tore at his hair,
His shoulders shook with sobbing, and he didn't see me there.

"Tell me please!" I said to him. "What's happened to our Lord?"
"Have they freed Him? Is He safe now? Have you any word?"

"I think there'll be a trial. He may even be condemned!
They mocked Him, and they beat Him--He who never sinned!"

"Three times they said I knew Him, and three times I denied.
He knows that I deserted Him, He knows how I have lied."

His tortured pain was worse than mine, regrets more than my own.
He demanded that I leave him there, to face his guilt alone.

I stayed close by, as did my mother, beating back my fear,
When would John return to us? And what were we to hear?

When John came back, he only said, "His trial's going on",
Mother nodded, then I followed, when Peter left with John.

I managed to catch up with them, dreading what I'd see!
I knew I loved the Master, and I knew that He loved me.

I saw Jesus in the courtyard, with Pilate staring down.
Despite the loud accusing cries, He uttered not a sound.

He stood there, weak and trembling; His blood ran down in streams.
His scourged and broken body would forever haunt my dreams.

I heard the sentence handed down, I heard the people roar!
Tears were running down my face, as I turned toward the door.

"Crucify--crucify" those words hung in the air!
I longed to go and help Him, and yet I didn't dare!

Soldiers dragged Him from the hall, into the crowded street.
I knew I had to follow Him, but I couldn't move my feet.

I saw Peter walking out, so I let him lead the way.
He would know what to do; he'd know what to say.

The soldiers pushed me roughly back, they wouldn't let me near,
And when I met the eyes of one, I felt a chilling fear.

Peter vanished in the crowd, and I searched in vain for John.
There was no one to follow now, but I made myself go on.

Far ahead, I saw the soldiers, gathering on the hill.
They'd dragged Him to that final place, to crucify and kill.

Jesus' life was being ended, by Caiaphas and Rome.
My mind felt numb, and then I saw, that I was walking home.

I found my mother waiting, I knew she had to hear!
When she learned these awful things, she would want me near.

Hours later, John appeared, with a woman in his care,
Her tortured face was streaked with tears, half covered by her hair.

"This is Mary," he softly said. "She's the mother of our Lord.
She's committed to my care. I have given Him my word."

Then others came and joined us, recounting all they'd seen;
Things so awful and unreal, it had be a dream.

I'd seen them load His shoulders with a heavy wooden cross.
Soon the wood was soaked and stained, with the blood that He had lost.

John said they drove their iron nails through His hands and feet,
And left Him dying on the cross for all the world to see.

Mary said that He forgave the ones who put Him there.
He promised heaven to a thief, when He had no breath to spare.

They told me all the words He spoke while He was nailed and torn.
I felt them as they pierced my mind, like sharp and angry thorns.

MY NAME IS MARK

"God, My Father, where are You? Why am I here alone?
Into your hands I give my spirit," then an awful gasping moan.

He sank down, His body limp, and then He closed His eyes.
"It is finished," came His whisper. And then came Mary's cries.

"The day became like night," they said, "and the awful shaking ground,"
"This truly was the son of God," was whispered all around.

They talked about the garden tomb, and why they laid Him there.
Important people knew Him, and now they seemed to care.

Mary looked away from us, her face was cold and still;
For now she had an emptiness, that none of us could fill.

I couldn't listen any more, the horror filled my head!
With my body tired and aching, I went away to bed.

I spent a fearful sleepless night, my body chilled and shaking.
The others seemed to be the same; first nightmare sleep, then waking.

Morning brought us no relief, the Sabbath brought no rest.
We were caught up in our grief, our lives could not be blessed.

Another endless hopeless night, with fitful nightmare sleep.
Fears and grief were intertwined with the watch that we must keep.

And then another dawning, the first day of the week;
A pounding on the door, jerked us from our sleep.

Were there soldiers waiting there, as they unlocked the door?
I thought about the crowd I'd seen, recalled their angry roar!

I saw that it was Mary, the one called Magdalene!
She was smiling as she came in, like someone in a dream!

"His tomb is empty! He's not there," Her voice was like a song.
"He stood alive before my eyes! I know that I'm not wrong!"

I still can hear John's loud cry as he ran from the room!
Peter followed after him. They were racing toward the tomb.

John came back and told us the stone was rolled away;
He was talking miracle, but I heard Peter say,

"Do I think that He's alive? Dozens watched Him die.
Can He bring Himself to life? Could either you or I?"

"Peter, He's the son of God!" John said loud and clear.
"God can raise up Jesus, or anyone that's here."

Peter still seemed full of guilt, still wore a face of doubt.
We all shared those feelings, and couldn't get them out.

That night I brought the food to them, then joined them at the table.
We tried to smile, tried to eat, though none of us were able.

Suddenly we saw a glow and then we saw a form;
Someone standing in the room, like sunlight bright and warm.

Then He was there, His arms outstretched, to gather us all in!
He was made of love and light, and we were doubt and sin.

None of us had stayed to help there in Gethsemane.
All of us had run away, our only thought to flee.

He suffered and He died for us, and now He rose again!
And here He stood loving us, after dying for our sin!

With a glance, His eyes met mine, and then sought Peter out.
I knew that He'd forgiven me, then I heard Peter's shout.

The love and peace in Peter's face, made him like a boy!
All of us were crowding round to touch and weep with joy.

What was new and wonderful, a glorious surprise!
Forever lay before us, as we looked into His eyes.

I knew I had to follow Him, knew I'd chosen right!
He lives and He is with me, however dark the night.

I was a boy of fifteen years and longed to serve a king.
Now my life belongs to Him, the King of everything!

"Peter preached and people came, there seemed to be no end.
There was power in the Spirit, that only God could send!"

*38 Then Peter said unto them, Repent, and be baptized every one of you
in the name of Jesus Christ for the remission of sins, and ye shall receive
the gift of the Holy Ghost.*

Acts 2:38 KJV

JOANNA
CHUZA'S WIFE

I went with the other women, to the tomb that day.
I know that He is risen and that He's still 'The Way'.

Before His death we followed Him, wherever He might lead.
Without Him here I often feel, much like a wind blown reed.

He used to tell us what to do, with a voice that I could hear.
Now I listen and I wonder if He is even near.

I think His mother hears Him speak; she smiles her quiet smile,
And the Magdalene says nothing, she just follows like a child.

And so I said to Chuza, what is there we can do?
He is gone and we must wait till He shows us something new.

It's true He walked among us, for many long sweet days!
Now the only word we have is--that we must sit and wait.

I wonder what we're waiting for; what could take His place?
There is no other Savior, we need to see His face!

The Pharisees are angry, they want us dead and gone;
They all looked like silly fools on that Resurrection dawn.

Chuza said to calm myself. Jesus always has a plan,
Whatever we are waiting for, that is in His hand.

A LAMB IS BORN

He said I should remember how God delivered me,
With just a word from Jesus, my soul has been set free.

I was possessed by demons like Mary Magdalene.
Chuza dragged me to our Lord, and begged that I be seen.

When I became myself again, I was there at Jesus' feet,
With my husband's arms around me, there in the dust and heat.

Hours and days of my life had vanished from my mind.
My husband still was faithful, and always he was kind.

We both chose to follow Him. We hung on His every word.
Our money went to care for Him, the man we called our Lord.

So we're waiting with the others until our orders come,
And we're going to see this through, till all the work is done.

Chuza stays quite busy, keeping Herod's household straight,
He hears the highest level news, of the Temple and the state.

We go quietly to the temple, to worship and to pray.
Still it's in this upper room the disciples like to stay.

It is there that we gather, to talk and reminisce.
We don't plan the future. We don't know what it is.

Still, yesterday we seemed to feel a gathering sense of power!
Something's going to happen, and it could be any hour.

Jesus said to us that day, that a comforter would come!
He wouldn't leave us orphans, with a mouth that's still and dumb.

He told us that we must go into the world and lead;
Bring other people to Him, that we must plant the seed.

And then He said to stay right here, in the upper room.
Something has to happen soon, or this will be our tomb.

JOANNA CHUZA'S WIFE

Peter hasn't gone to fish; he's doing as he's told.
He's not the same old Peter! He's anything but bold!

John looks very thoughtful. He sometimes nods his head,
As though he has remembered, something the Lord has said.

We spent the evening here last night, in the upper room;
Praying all together that something changes soon.

We prayed and talked, and talked and prayed, until the morning came.
And we felt a certain knowing that nothing was the same.

None of us ate breakfast. We had no appetite,
We were seeking the will of God, just as we had all night.

The air around us shimmered, as if with flecks of gold.
Our spirits were rejoicing to watch God's will unfold.

We joined hands and hearts together. Our voices were like one.
Joy and faith washed over us, as warming as the sun.

From somewhere in the room, we began to hear a sound,
Like the whisper of a breeze, that murmurs all around.

The sound came through the window; it surged in through the door.
We were all a part of it, we could feel the mighty roar.

The voice of God was speaking; we heard it everyone!
God's presence was inside us, we were glowing like the sun!

A burning tongue had come to rest on each and every head;
We laughed and cried and spoke aloud, not knowing what we said.

Peter laughed and shouted as he was running down the stair!
He began to preach to everyone, once he reached the open air.

We all followed Peter out into the street!
All our fears had vanished. The very air was sweet!

As Peter preached his message, we began to walk around,
We smiled and talked of Jesus to everyone we found!

People gathered to us, they listened and they heard;
No matter what their language, they understood each word.

Some people said they thought, 'we'd had too much to drink,'
We told them, 'It's still morning! This isn't what you think!'

People came from everywhere when they heard Peter's voice.
He told them they were sinners, and he told them to rejoice.

He told them Jesus loved them! He told them loud and clear!
He said that Jesus came to save them, and they had no need for fear.

He told them Jesus died for them, and that He rose again!
He said they only must believe, and repent of all their sin!

Soon there were hundreds there, all kneeling in the street.
The Spirit spoke through Peter, and brought them to belief.

Peter preached and people came, there seemed to be no end.
There was power in the Spirit, that only God could send!

Peter preached for hours; thousands listened and believed,
Jews from every nation, from every tongue and creed.

And still the glory stayed on us, and set us all apart,
We were doing the work of God, and He was in our heart.

All of us brought people into the kingdom of our Lord,
New people who could go out, and help us spread the Word.

Our fears all were gone now, our hearts were set aglow!
This was the Holy Spirit, this was Jesus in our soul.

When the day was over, and we sought the upper room;
We saw it was our cradle, it never was a tomb.

We laughed together at the fears, that used to hold us back.
Now our souls had the courage that we used to lack.

Soon now, God will send us forth to tell the world the news.
There is a life we've given up; we all have had to choose.

But now there is a New Life, living in our souls.
Through the Holy Spirit, God has made us whole.

I will go with Chuza wherever God may send us.
Using all our talents, whatever God may lend us.

Jesus was One Person, dwelling in one time and place.
We will scatter everywhere, wearing Jesus' face.

"The rocks came at him in a frenzy, of evil killing hate,
Stephen fell before them, yet their rage did not abate."

*58 And cast him out of the city, and stoned him: and the witnesses laid
down their clothes at a young man's feet, whose name was Saul.
59 And they stoned Stephen, calling upon God, and saying, Lord Jesus,
receive my spirit.*

Acts 7:58, 59 KJV

STEPHEN

ACTS 6 AND 7

The first time I saw Stephen, he seemed a gentle man,
Kind to everyone he met, with an open giving hand.

He joined with us at Pentecost when the Holy Spirit came,
And we all became one body, trusting in God's name.

I grew so fond of Stephen; he seemed like a son to me.
My heart was very joyful that our friendship came to be.

Stephen was a strong support as we worked and carried on,
He always did what Peter asked, but his closest friend was John,

We shared everything together. We cared for those in need,
We knew we were one body, in thought and word and deed.

The disciples kept to praying and preaching in the street.
But it happened that some widows hadn't got enough to eat.

These women were of Greek descent, still they were no less Jews.
Now they followed Jesus, and they had just as much to lose.

The disciples spoke together. The problem must be met.
And so they chose the seven, to even up the debt.

Stephen was the first they picked, for he would understand.
Stephen was a Greek himself, living in our Hebrew land.

Stephen was the first of seven, and the rest were also Greeks.
They bought supplies and gave out food, so everyone could eat.

Stephen worked hard at his new job. He liked to organize,
And if it was a big job, he didn't mind the size.

It wasn't long until the deacons made everything run smooth;
So there was time for him to preach, to tell the world the truth.

Stephen loved the preaching! he loved to speak to crowds.
He loved to talk of Jesus, loved to say His name out loud.

He was filled with the Holy Spirit, and he healed in Jesus name,
He preached the Gospel message, teaching everyone who came.

"Follow me," Jesus said, "each day take up your cross,
Be sure they'll persecute you for there always is a cost".

Teaching truth, and miracles, brought people to 'the way';
But many grew to hate him, and what he had to say.

We'd walked through this with Jesus; now it all began again.
The truth, we found, is always feared by evil doing men.

One synagogue came forth with loud and angry cries,
"Blasphemy", they shouted out, "this man deserves to die!"

We'd seen it all before, not so very long ago.
Could it happen here once more? I prayed it wasn't so.

Stephen kept on preaching, kept his eyes upon the goal.
One man named Saul took notice, with venom in his soul.

And so, when Stephen preached out in the public square,
A crowd was gathered up, and they arrested him right there.

He was taken to the council, where he must defend himself.
After praying to the Father, he knew there would be help.

STEPHEN

We all prayed for Stephen; we trusted in God's plan.
We said "We'll be there with you, to help you if we can".

Stephen stood before the council without a trace of fear,
He had a chance to tell them the things he held most dear.

Stephen preached a long time. Some people were in awe.
Some thought it wasn't Stephen, but an angel that they saw!

He talked about the people, and how they had been warned.
He talked about the prophets, and how they had been scorned,

He told how God loved them, and how they turned away!
He told them all the wondrous things, that Jesus had to say.

He told them God had sent His son, but He was crucified.
He told them Jesus rose again, after He had died!

Looking up to heaven, Stephen's face began to glow.
He was saying all the things God wanted them to know.

The Holy Spirit filled him; I could see the tongue of fire.
The council began to scream at him, they said he was a liar!

Stephen said above him, he could see the Son of Man.
Jesus, he said, was standing, there at God's right hand!

I looked up to heaven, thinking I might see this too.
Instantly, I could see, what Stephen said was true.

The council screamed out "blasphemy," covering up their ears,
Grabbing hold, they dragged him out, with loud and angry jeers.

They took him from the city, led by a man named Saul.
That they would now stone Stephen, was shouted by them all.

Saul stood by to watch their coats, as they gathered up their stones.
They kept looking back at Stephen, expecting cries and moans.

A LAMB IS BORN

We watched Stephen from close by, all of us who came,
And what we saw we'd not forget, for he suffered in God's name.

Stephen began to pray aloud, in a gentle steady voice.
He spoke to God about these men, and he spoke about their choice.

And then one man filled with hate cast out his first stone!
Still, I prayed that they would stop, and leave our friend alone.

Those awful stones began to fly, coming thick and fast!
Through this awful hail of rock, our Stephen couldn't last.

The rocks came at him in a frenzy, of evil killing hate!
Stephen fell before them, yet their rage did not abate.

The man named Saul with twisted smile, saw what the mob had done.
I looked for pity in his face, but his staring eyes showed none.

Stephen lay there dying, in that brutal rain of stone;
Couldn't they just leave him there, to go to God alone?

I crept as close to my dying friend as I dared to go,
He closed his eyes a moment, as the hail began to slow.

Then once more he raised his head, and opened up his eyes.
"Father, please forgive them," he said, looking to the skies.

"Lord Jesus take my spirit home." Peace was in his face.
I was wishing in that moment, that I could take his place.

Their evil work was now complete, and the mob just walked away.
We, who were his closest friends, knew that God would have us stay.

We picked him up and carried him, as gently as we could.
In death he now belonged to God, as some sweet day we would.

My heart was glad for Stephen. I was sure in death, he'd won,
I knew that somewhere Stephen was rejoicing with my Son.

"Will you lead me to Damascus?" I asked the men with me,
"I have learned this very hour that it's where I need to be."

*8 And Saul arose from the earth; and when his eyes were opened,
he saw no man: but they led him by the hand, and brought him into
Damascus.*

Acts 9:8 KJV

SAUL OF TARSUS

I stood and watched Stephen die, right there in front of me.
I told myself that it was right, what he said was blasphemy.

I never said a word myself, I never threw a stone.
I just told myself he'd sinned, and now he must atone.

I heard him ask forgiveness, for those who struck him down,
For those who had tried him, and dragged him out of town.

I stood and watched him close his eyes, and show no sign of fear.
I just stood and watched the coats, for those who brought him here,

I stood and watched Stephen die, then I just walked away,
We had to stop these people! We had to make them pay.

I went back to the temple, and met with some Pharisees.
The Sanhedrin listened to my plan, and they agreed with me.

These followers of Jesus, we must go and hunt them down.
We can't allow this Jesus talk, to spread to other towns!

In a week or maybe two, I had the warrants in my hand,
I surely thought that all would go, exactly as I planned.

I'd go out to Damascus first; there's a group that's gathered there.
They must be arrested now, or we haven't got a prayer.

A LAMB IS BORN

It was a long hot journey, but I knew it must be done,
This Jesus had convinced them that he was the promised one.

I knew it would go smoothly. We'd taken every care.
I brought some others with me; I'd need some help out there,

We traveled out on horseback; it was too far to walk.
We didn't spare the horses, and had little time for talk.

I thought about my mission! I mustn't let myself be kind.
Stephen's final dying words mustn't come into my mind.

I refused to think of Stephen! I would dwell on what was right!
Rooting out this Jesus cult was where I'd set my sight.

Damascus was drawing near, and the sun grew very hot.
We led the horses for a while, and looked for a shady spot.

There had been a little breeze to cool my sweaty brow.
That died down, an hour ago, and the sun was blazing now.

I never saw the sun so bright; it burned into my eyes,
But the light I saw was not the sun, for it covered up the sky.

I kept on walking for a while, but my shaking knees gave way.
An awful fear had gripped my heart, and I couldn't even pray.

I lay there on the dusty road, Damascus was so near!
The blinding light enveloped me, thunder filled my ear!

"Saul," I heard, "I want to know, why you do me hurt?"
"You hate and persecute me, now you tremble in the dirt."

"Who are you, Lord," I quavered, afraid of what I'd hear!
My mind was saying, 'Stephen' and it filled me full of fear.

I could see a tall bright figure, from which the light had come!
I could only stare in wonder, and the wonder struck me dumb.

SAUL OF TARSUS

"I am Jesus," was what I heard, there lying on the road,
"For you it seems to be too hard, to kick against the goads."

I knew what He was saying, and I knew that this was true.
I never asked if I was right, or what God would have me do.

In a flash I clearly saw the wrongs that I had done;
I knew concerning mercy, for me there should be none!

I saw here the living Jesus that the Romans crucified.
It was true what Stephen said; it was for me he died!

"What shall I do now, Lord," What could I give to Him?
What would be the consequence of my black and awful sin?

"Get up, Saul, get on your feet, and remember what I say;
Go into Damascus and there you'll find the way."

"Someone in the city will come and talk to you.
He will have instructions and tell you what to do."

Jesus then departed, vision faded, and was gone.
Now no light could hurt my eyes, darkness blocked the sun.

I didn't hit my eyes or head when I took my fall,
But when they helped me up again, I couldn't see at all!

My fellow travelers realized, I'd become quite blind!
We hardly knew each another, but they helped me and were kind.

All of my companions were amazed and full of fear,
Jesus' voice had fallen like thunder on their ears.

"Will you lead me to Damascus?" I asked the men with me,
"I have learned this very hour that it's where I need to be."

They took me to the city, to an inn where I could stay.
I thought perhaps I'd spend my life, just learning how to pray.

A LAMB IS BORN

Then I found I had no will to either eat or drink,
The only thing I wanted was to ponder and to think.

I remembered Stephen, and what we did to him;
I thought about Jesus, and I thought about my sin.

It seemed so very strange, that now I could not see;
Inside, I finally understood how blind I used to be.

I wondered what the Lord would be telling me to do.
I was blind and helpless, and that He surely knew.

In that dark regretting place that had become my life;
In a dream I saw a man, who would give me back my sight.

Ananias was the man I dreamed was at the door,
He put forth a healing hand, and I could see once more.

Sure enough, it wasn't long till he came and entered in.
He knew exactly who I was, and he knew my every sin.

"Saul," he said, "I've come to you at our Lord's request.
You have lived half your live, you owe to God the rest."

"You must be Spirit filled," he said, "You must be born anew.
It's time that you forget your past. God has work for you to do."

Then he laid his hands on me, and he began to pray.
Soon I could see the darkened room, and then I saw his face.

The room grew bright and brighter, as my vision was restored.
I began to weep and speak strange words, in the glory of the Lord.

Ananias stayed with me till I was healed and whole,
Then he said some words to me that were precious to my soul.

"I know you, Saul of Tarsus. I know why you came here.
We did not want to trust you, you only brought us fear."

"I know that you met Jesus on that hot and dusty road;
And so I call you Brother, and I ask to share your load.

The same Lord and Savior, you met three days ago,
Said I had to tell you all the things I know.

The Lord has chosen you for work that must be done.
You will go throughout the world to tell them of God's son.

You will preach to Gentiles, you will speak to kings,
You will travel through the world, to talk about these things."

I was feeling faint with hunger; they brought me food to eat,
When I had finished and grown stronger, I got up on my feet.

"Please baptize me with water, I've repented and been cleansed.
I'd like to come and meet the others. I need to talk to them."

I thought they wouldn't want me; perhaps they'd turn away.
Still I had to go to them, there were many debts to pay.

I'll stay here in Damascus, till God gives me further call.
I also have to change my name. Now I'll be known as Paul.

I stood and watched Stephen die; I can close my eyes and see,
He is there lying at my feet, but his mantle rests on me.

"The brothers planned to sneak him out through the city wall.
He came over in a basket, or he'd not be here at all."

*24 But their laying await was known of Saul. And they watched the
gates day and night to kill him.
25 Then the disciples took him by night, and let him down by the wall
in a basket.*

Acts 9:24,25 KJV

PAUL AND BARNABAS

Saul of Tarsus came to me. He said to call him 'Paul'.
He said he had a story, and that he would tell me all.

He'd gone to Peter years ago, but Peter would not hear.
Saul said that he fully understood, the apostles' doubts and fear.

I looked at Saul of Tarsus--'Paul', I could not say.
I asked him why he came to me; what fear could I allay?

He said there were happenings that completely changed his life.
He said the things he used to do, now cut him like a knife.

He said that he met Jesus, and was blinded by the light.
He said he chose to follow Him, and was given back his sight.

The brothers in Damascus brought him to 'the way',
He was sheltered by the body there, as long as he could stay.

He preached in all the synagogues, saying 'Jesus is God's son',
He told them all his story, and confessed the things he'd done.

The Jews knew Saul of Tarsus; they felt angry and betrayed.
They searched their city for him, and watched the city gates.

The brothers planned to sneak him out through the city wall.
He came over in a basket, or he'd not be here at all.

He hid in another kingdom till things had settled down.
He'd waited till the Lord had called him, then came back to town.

Before me was the man I'd seen with hatred in his eyes,
Who watched them stoning Stephen, and never looked aside.

This was the man who led the Jews to hunt believers down.
He was planning death or prison for all of us he found.

I looked at this man closely, he really seemed to care;
But my heart remembered Stephen, I could see him lying there.

"Saul," I said, "I have to think. Even more, I have to pray.
Come to me tomorrow. I'll know what God would have me say".

"I'll come," he said quite simply, with lowered head and eyes.
"Pray to God and ask Him, for I know what He'll reply."

I spent the evening praying, then prayed all through the night.
I didn't want to trust this man, but I understood his plight.

By morning I was tired and worn, I'd argued and God won.
I knew that God had chosen him; he had a race to run.

When Saul returned next morning, I met him with a smile.
I knew he was an honest man, that in him was no guile.

"Saul," I said, "I've talked to God, and He has calmed my heart.
Come, let us go to Peter. Now, I'm prepared to do my part."

I took him to Jerusalem, and found Peter there and John.
John reached out his hand to us; Peter told us to be gone.

"Peter," I said firmly, "you know that I have prayed.
Saul belongs to Jesus now, and we have to let him stay."

Peter put aside his anger, and he looked us through and through,
His smile was warm and open. "What would you have me do?"

"Just listen to him, Peter. There are things he needs to tell,
Jesus chose him as He did you, and leads him just as well."

Big rough Peter now sat down next to little Saul.
Peter listened as he talked, and liked him after all.

I saw Peter start to smile, as he listened to Saul talk.
Peter forgives quickly; he remembers his own faults!

John and Peter took to Saul, and the brothers followed after,
When we first broke bread with him, we heard some nervous laughter.

Saul was such a friend to us, as though he'd been for years.
His mind was seeking and intense; he had no time for fears.

He debated with the Jews, to bring them to the truth.
He had met and talked to Jesus; he had seen the living proof!

I think somehow Stephen's death still came before his eyes.
All sin must be repented, and this he realized.

The vicious hate that fell on Stephen, was soon to fall on Saul,
His former friendships in the temple-- helped him not at all.

Saul, himself, had no fear; he preached of a risen Lord.
But the anger he was stirring up, his friends could not afford.

The word was out in Jerusalem that Saul would have to die.
We didn't want another martyr; we had better say good bye.

I knew God had commissioned Saul, and he had to stay alive!
If the Jews should kill him now, the world would be deprived.

So I went to Saul and told him, it was better that he go.
I'd get him safely to a place, that only he would know.

Saul was an honest upright man, he knew that we were right,
He said "I'll go to Tarsus, and I will stay out of sight."

We went to Caesarea and the brothers left him there,
I sailed with him to Tarsus, where he found a house to share.

Saul was humbly mending tents when I saw him last.
He knew that God would call him when the danger passed.

The persecution that we had after Stephen had been lost,
Caused many to leave the city, or death would be the cost!

Now there were settlements of believers through the land,
Teaching Jews a message they could love and understand.

Years passed by and 'the way' was accepted, and it grew.
I wondered how Saul was faring, but I never really knew.

Some believers did more than this; they began to talk with Greeks.
In Antioch, where I had gone, it was time for Saul to preach.

And so I went to Tarsus, I went to find my friend.
I rejoiced that Saul was waiting, at my journey's end.

And there he was in Tarsus, teaching men as he made tents!
He was sharing with believers, his faith and his good sense.

I opened my arms and my heart, to this man whose faith was true.
He greeted me with a question, "What would you have me do?"

"It's time to do God's work, my friend, for He has made a path.
He will go ahead of you. You don't even have to ask.

Foreign lands and foreign kings, God is lord of all,
We will do these things together, my own dear brother, Paul."

Cover art is by award winning artist, Stewart Sherwood. Mr. Sherwood is a native of Toronto, Ontario, and his creativity has found expression in many different media. He has done celebrity portraits, limited edition collectible art, commemorative coins, illustrations, and television promotions. Mr. Sherwood's warm and inspirational work can be viewed at www.stewartsherwood.ca